UNDERSTANDING AND MANAGING YOUR TEMPER

Navigating emotional storms, and attaining inner peace, and emotional stability in health, marriage, and enterprise

ALEXANDER ZABADINO

Copyright © 2024 Alexander Zabadino

All rights reserved. No part of this book may be reproduced or transmitted in any form or by any means, electronic or mechanical, including photocopying, recording or by any means information storage and retrieval system without prior permission of the author.

This book is a work of non-fiction. The views are solely those of the author, and do not necessarily reflect the views of the publisher and thereby disclaims any responsibility for them.

Table of Contents

INTRODUCTION 6

DEFINING THE HUMAN TEMPER. 11

    How can we describe a bad Temper? 19

CAUSES OF A BAD TEMPER 22

REASONS WHY YOU NEED TO DEAL WITH YOUR TEMPER. 29

THE RELATIONSHIP BETWEEN SIN AND TEMPERAMENT. 35

TURNING AWAY WRATH 39

THE HUMAN TEMPER AND LIFE'S JOURNEY. 42

    Neonates. 42

    Children. 43

    Teenagers. 44

TEMPERAMENT IN THE YOUTH. 50

CONQUERING BAD TEMPER AND ACHIEVING SUCCESS IN YOUR MARITAL JOURNEY. 55

    The first five years of marriage. 56

TEMPER IN THE SIXTH TO TENTH YEARS OF MARRIAGE. 62

HANDLING TEMPER ISSUES IN THE ELEVENTH AND FIFTEENTH YEARS INTO MARRIAGE. 67

THE IMPACT OF A BAD TEMPER IN THE WORKPLACE AND PRODUCTIVITY. 71

How do we manage temperament in bosses? 71

Managing issues with colleagues................................74

Managing temperament in the subordinates. 75

Managing self temperament. 77

Ten scriptures that highlight the importance of counselling and seeking wisdom: 79

THE IMPACT OF TEMPERAMENT ON PHYSICAL AND MENTAL HEALTH..81

The four major types of temperament are; sanguine, cholera, melancholic, and phlegmatic. 82

Sanguine personality..82

The health vulnerabilities of a sanguine personality 83

Choleric personality..84

The health vulnerabilities of a choleric personality 85

Melancholic personality...87

The health vulnerabilities of a melancholic personality. 88

Phlegmatic personality 89

The health vulnerabilities of phlegmatic personalities. 91

STRESS MANAGEMENT 93

What is stress? 93

Stress and its impact. 93

What are common approaches to stress management?..............94

GENERAL OVERVIEW ON TEMPER MANAGEMENT 101

INTRODUCTION

The human temper is potentially a wild animal, but it takes your relationship with Jesus Christ, and the knowledge of God's word and your ability to apply God's word for you to tame the wild animal referred to as the temper.

We can accurately say that your outcomes are a product of your temper, and you may not be able to please God and enjoy his promises, if you cannot control a bad temper. The Bible says in Psalm 51:16-17,

[16]for thou desire not sacrifice; else would I give it: thou delighted not in burnt offering. [17]the sacrifices of God are a broken spirit: a broken and a contrite heart, O God, thou wilt not despise.

The problems of many people today are rooted in a lack of self control, over their temper, unbelievers and believers alike. When you have a bad temper, it is difficult for you to be an effective leader, in the workplace. It is also difficult for you to patiently explain your product to potential customers, and may lose them somewhere along the line.

To be a good husband or wife, you equally need to have a good temper, otherwise there would be quarrels, and contentions regularly, which may lead to irreconcilable differences and a divorce, for example, when the trials of this life come knocking.

The temper also has a role to pray in times of sickness, and the management of healthcare for hospital staff and other categories of care staff. When the temper is out of control, symptoms like headache, depression, anxiety and sleeplessness are common. The melancholic individual may exhibit these characteristics, whilst the sanguine may remain lively or indifferent. There are four major personality traits, known as the Sanguine, Choleric, Melancholic, and Phlegmatic. We shall examine the different characteristics of each group in a later chapter.

Productivity in the work place correlates with the ability to manage the temperament. There are different tendencies that could be displayed in the place of work, as by leaders, colleagues and subordinates. Some are lazy, incorrigible, cannot work without supervision, late comers to work and so on. How do we deal with people and maintain peace and optimal productivity under these circumstances?

As a servant of God, or a believer, you must learn to attain mastery over your destiny, by controlling your temper. The Bible says in the book of

Proverbs 25:28

He that hath no rule over his own spirit is like a city that is broken down, and without walls.

It therefore follows that all that the enemy needs to do to attack you or ravage your destiny, is to provoke you to anger, and once you lose your temper, you have fallen flat before the enemy. Likewise, all you need to do to prevent the weapons of the enemies from prospering against your life is to guard your spirit against provocation and losing your temper.

In Psalm 39:1, David laments

¹I said, I will take heed to my ways, that I sin not with my tongue; I will keep my mouth with a bridle, while the wicked is before me

² I was dumb with silence, I held my peace, even from good; and my sorrow was stirred.

³ My heart was hot within me, while I was musing, the fire burned: then spake I with my tongue.

In this book, we shall try to uncover what temper is and seek to establish an understanding of the subject, what causes anger, the relationship between your temper and how it affects holy living, the impact of anger, on physical, mental and spiritual health, the physiological aspects of anger, and in broad terms, how to manage your temper, and live the type of life that God wants you to live.

It is good to note that the destinies of many have been waiting for a book like this to restore understanding and peace to their marriages. Many leaders need to get their workers to read the material in this book in order to work peacefully with one another and enhance productivity. Certainly, the results this year shall be better than the last year.

Many parents are not aware that their children's woes are as acres ultimate of their provocation. This is why the bible encourages in

Ephesians 6:4

And ye fathers, provoke not your children to wrath: but bring them up in the nurture and admonition of the Lord.

When husband and wife are not able to control their temper, there will be a communication problem, and decision making will suffer. It is then difficult to bring every good purpose to manifestation because the house is in disorder. It is a terrible problem whose consequences are being under-estimated. How do couples react, when the financial and emotional burdens increase? When a partner loses his or her job, or at the later stages of life, when geriatric changes give way to malady, how do the couples behave. A thorough knowledge of these tendencies are necessary to be able to navigate through these possibilities.

A bad temper is usually not an occurrence, but usually becomes a lifestyle that may plant itself in the sub-conscious mind of a victim and affect every aspect of human life. Mostly affected is the health of the individual. In a practical sense, someone with a bad temper cannot enjoy good health, if the World Health Organisation's (WHO) definition of health is anything to go by. The WHO defines health as a complete state of physical, mental and social wellbeing, and not just the absence of infirmity or disease. As we go through this book, you shall discover certain secrets that will take you to the next level in the fulfilment of your ambitions. Wish you a happy reading.

CHAPTER ONE

DEFINING THE HUMAN TEMPER.

Temper can be defined as a person's state of mind seen in terms of their being angry or calm.

A bad human temper is one of the most destructive characteristics of the human being, usually a snappy temper, responds to life's situations irrationally. It makes man to lose control, commit errors, fall onto temptation, rebel against God, and condemnation. An inability to control the temper is a fertiliser to sin, iniquity, and every evil work. An example that readily comes to mind is in Numbers 20:10-13

Numbers 20:7-12

⁷And the LORD spake unto Moses, saying,

⁸Take the rod, and gather thou the assembly together, thou, and Aaron thy brother, and speak ye unto the rock before their eyes; and it shall give forth his water, and thou shalt bring forth to them water out of the rock: so, thou shalt give the congregation and their beasts drink.

⁹And Moses took the rod from before the LORD, as he commanded him.

[10]And Moses and Aaron gathered the congregation together before the rock, and he said unto them, hear now, ye rebels; must we fetch you water out of this rock?

[11]And Moses lifted up his hand, and with his rod he smote the rock twice: and the water came out abundantly, and the congregation drank, and their beasts also.

[12]And the LORD spake unto Moses and Aaron, because ye believed me not, to sanctify me in the eyes of the children of Israel, therefore ye shall not bring this congregation into the land which I have given them.

This is a case of a bad temper, and we can see the instruction, response and effect in the life of Moses. He was instructed by God to speak to the rock before their eyes; and it shall give forth his water, and he shall bring forth to them bring forth to them water. Sometimes, the things we see around us, our relationships with people, how they react to us, our expectations from people, our experiences in the past, our woes, our failures, how satisfied we are with ourselves, financial status could come between us and the love of Christ that we may misbehave. However, in Romans 8:35

Romans 8:35-39

³⁵Who shall separate us from the love of Christ? shall tribulation, or distress, or persecution, or famine, or nakedness, or peril, or sword?

³⁶as it is written, for thy sake we are killed all the day long; we are accounted as sheep for the slaughter.

³⁷Nay, in all these things we are more than conquerors through him that loved us.

³⁸For I am persuaded, that neither death, nor life, nor angels, nor principalities, nor powers, nor things present, nor things to come,

³⁹nor height, nor depth, nor any other creature, shall be able to separate us from the love of God, which is in Christ Jesus our Lord.

Verses 35 and 36 suggest that irrespective of anything at all that may befall us, we should try to withstand and be resilient, just because of the love of Christ. No experience, feeling or imagination should come between us and our determination to do that which is right in the light of the scriptures, no matter who offends us or whatsoever they do. We agree that people may hurt us or disappoint us. We should try to be patient in tribulation (Romans 12:12-15).

A man told his wife that he was going to work, one morning, and said bye to her. He got to the office, and discovered that he forgot something at home. He went back home to fetch what he forgot. Alas, on getting home, he went straight to his bedroom hurriedly as the door was not locked. The wife was not expecting anyone at that time, since the husband just left. He met the love of his life, and a strange man in the very act of sexual intimacy and pleasure, in their bedroom and on the matrimonial bed! If you were that man, what would you do, under the circumstances. Remember, the bible says, "be angry but sin not".

In another instance, a woman forgot something at home and came back to pick it. She got to the house, and met her best friend on bed with her husband. If you were the woman, what would you do? There was this other person, who was living abroad and committed his building project into the hands of his elder brother. He came back home only to discover that the pictures his elder brother has been sending were actually fake. He was spending the money. What would you do, if you were at the receiving end. You may probably shout, fight, and be tempted to do something crazy. But wait, does that solve the problem in any way? No. If no, then is it worth it to do something silly? No, it is not. Then why act irrationally?

When we are tempted to lose our temper, maturity demands that we try and do something that will restore and bring back our temper. Most times, you walk away quietly and think about the solution. That is better! In the case of the man above, who caught his wife in the very act, he said nothing, but walked away! He came back home later after the days work. The wife was now feeling very uncomfortable. Silence is golden, sometimes. That is why God says you should hold your peace, and he will fight for you! It returns the shame to the offender. One day, in Ijora, Lagos, under the bridge, I was being harassed by some street urchins. I kept quiet and continued going my way. When it was too much, some passers by came to my rescue, and gave those boys the discipline they lacked. God used them to fight for me. If I reacted, they could have attacked and molested me. When you are provoked extremely, one of the greatest reactions you could ever show is to summon the courage to keep quiet.

An abusive partner may charge and rant all day. Make sure you give brief explanations at least to maintain the communication, but try as much as possible to control your temper. Instead of arguing, you could go inside to sleep or do some other beneficial things, or excuse yourself to out. A temperate person is a powerful person. We should learn to keep our body under subjection.

1 Corinthians 9:27

But I keep under my body, and bring it into subjection: lest that by any means, when I have preached to others, I myself should be a cast away.

Generally, we can have a good (even) temper, or a bad (short) temper. A good temper is pleasant and most desirable. It is the attribute of champions. A bad temper can release its venom and destroy at anytime, if it is not tamed. The human temperament is so dangerous that the reaction does not have to be violent to be lethal. A bad temper can manifest in our attitudes or decisions and to linger for a long time. For example;

1 Samuel 18:6-9

⁶and it came to pass as they came, when David was returned from the slaughter of the Philistine, that the women came out of all cities of Israel, singing and dancing, to meet king Saul, with tabrets, with joy, and with instruments of music.

⁷and the women answered one another as they played, and said, Saul hath slain his thousands, and David his ten thousand.

⁸And Saul was very wroth, and the saying displeased him; and he said, they have ascribed unto David ten thousand, and to me they have ascribed but thousands: and what can he have more but the kingdom?

⁹And Saul eyed David from that day and forward.

The bible tells us in verse 8, that Saul was very wroth, which other Bible translations express as very angry! But he couldn't do anything violent in that instance, except that in verse 9, he could only eye him from that day and forward. That incident provoked a temperament in Saul, and I can't just imagine how he felt anytime he saw David or what his inner feelings were.

Someone may keep quiet and pause in reaction to a disappointing attitude from someone, but be subtly temperamental. Even though they don't talk, the fire is burning from inside. A husband and wife were discussing an issue on the telephone, and all of a sudden, one of them was quiet for a while, and after a few minutes of silence, the other line went dead. The other person calls again, and asks, what the matter was, but the response was "nothing". From that time, his changed in the household and the relationship was affected. Sometimes, such mistakes escalate to a divorce eventually.

Most temperamental issues in most homes are due to a shirking of responsibilities. It is good for you to pay attention to minute details in order to be able to address temperament. I have counselled men and women who had terrible issues of temperament in their marriages. By the time you will get to the root of the matter, it all boils down to denial of conjugal rights (sex). Many men have grown wild for that simple reason and may not be healed soon. I listened with sympathy to a woman, who said that her husband denies her sex for as long as six months sometimes. Why? He started suspecting she was a witch after 3 kids. So ridiculous! The house was always in turmoil until that was rectified.

Another issue that raises a bad temper is financial issues. It is either that one of the parties is not transparent about money or they decided to hide their payslips. There was a woman I knew many years ago. Her principle and belief were that no matter how small her salary was, the husband was not entitled to see the payslip. The man grew wild and temperamental, until the woman came to me. I counselled her to show him the payslip, because she was having what she didn't bargain foe. There was instant peace in the house.

An employer who is in debt and is funding it difficult to break even in business will always have temper issues. He will always unleash his anger uncontrollably over the staff. However, this is counterproductive and will only worsen the case. A bad temperament creates and atmosphere of fear and reduced productivity. It is a time to look at motivational strategies and not to

How can we describe a bad Temper?

1. It is over speeding on the highway of destiny.
2. When the zoo keeper damns the consequences and releases the lion in the midst of the spectators.
3. It is hitting the rock twice when you are to hit once
4. It is the attitude that makes one to lose instead of possessing
5. Injecting your spirit with a poison making you to behave irrationally.
6. It is temporary display of insanity.
7. Handing over the steering will of your emotions and actions to the devil.
8. When you open the door of your life to the condemnation of your enemies

9. When you cannot hold your spiritual vomit and you let it loose on yourself and others.
10. A bad temper is the hidden hand that is pushing you to commit error.
11. It is the sharp sword you have allowed to destroy great things in your life.
12. It is the evil storm you allow to rage against your destiny.
13. It is the internal serpent bitting you and making you to lose dominion.
14. Demonstrating a bad temper is an attempt to close the door against the good things God has planned for your life.
15. The permission you have given to the devil to stop your glorious manifestation in the market square of your life.
16. It is the evil shield you use to prevent your open heavens.
17. It is the act of removing heavens protection and uncovering yourself for the enemy's attacks.
18. It is the decision to put on the garment of shame and reproach in spite A of all the warnings.
19. A bad temper is pointing the gun against yourself and pulling the trigger.
20. A bad temper is a fall down a steep slope.
21. It is the revival of the spirit of self destruction.

22. It is the consuming fire you use to set your coat of many colours ablaze.
23. It is intentionally leaving the brakes unapplied when you are faced with an impending collision.
24. It is shutting the door of your sitting room and throwing the key into the swimming pool.
25. It is rolling in the mud because you were offended.
26. Opening the jar called you and spilling out the contents called your innermost secrets.
27. A bad temper is the evil smoke that follows you everywhere, making people to wonder.
28. It is inability to be able to put yourself under subjection.
29. It is pouring out the baby with the bath water.
30. A fire in you that burns and makes you to utter the things you shouldn't have uttered.

CHAPTER 2

CAUSES OF A BAD TEMPER

Reacting irrationally to perceived threats, offences, misdemeanours, and all sorts of wrong behaviour or attitude.

Behaviour can be due to a variety of factors from different origins. It may be as a result of certain things as a result of a person's sin, other people's sin and negligence, or just merely circumstances in the environment beyond our control. These causes include

1. Misconceived thoughts and imaginations from the victim. Sometimes, we mean what other people do not mean or say. As a result of this, we tend to react and boil within us, just because there was a gap in understanding or conception. This could in turn lead us to misbehave. When your reaction exceeds a certain expectation or normal reasoning, then it could be referred to as a bad temper.
2. Unforgiveness is another cause. When someone has offended you, but you are so angered that you refuse to find something to justify their actions, it may lead to a bad temper. In Luke 23:24, the accusers of Jesus ill treated him, but he found a reason to forgive them as he said, father forgive them for they know not what they do. The

reason was simple! They were ignorant of the inappropriateness and consequences of the things that they did. This included Judas but it did not exclude them from being punished by God.

3. Pride and arrogance resulting from an elated ego could make you feel angered and temperamental. Jesus advises us that the sure approach is to humble ourselves that we may be exalted. 1 Peter 5:6 says, "Therefore, humble yourself under the mighty hand of God that he may exalt you in due time". It doesn't matter who offended you or what they did. The word of God encourages us to humble ourselves. Similarly, God declares that we should hold our peace,

4. Emotions of fear or doubt could also result in a short temper, or bad temper. When you are afraid of an impending situation, and doubting your wellbeing or safety for no fault of yours, but other people's faults, it could result in a bad temper, as you seem to over-react. The Bible says in Ecclesiastes 7:7 that oppression makes a wise man mad.

5. Failure is another factor that may cause a bad temper. It is difficult to accept failure and downgrade, irrespective of the cause. This may linger for sometime, and for as long as

it lingers, there is a rise in temperament. It is inevitable that sometimes we face circumstances that connote failure or drawback. If this happens, we need to know that it has an expiry date, and is not forever. We should work hard, trusting and believing God and everything shall be okay.

6. Stress is a major cause of a short temper and a bad temper. There are different causes of stress, and the manifestations are diverse. If someone can manage anger effectively, then it is possible to deal with many demonic influences without any problems. Stress in itself causes illness and controlling illness translates to healing physically, mentally or emotionally. Uncontrolled emotions could strengthen demons and lead to terrible consequences affecting the wellbeing itself. It is difficult enjoying your Christian life when you are undergoing stress.

7. Unfair treatment. When someone is not treated fairly compared to others, he or she may be temperamental. It is good to treat our staff and other co-workers fairly in order to enhance peace and productivity.

8. Lack of sleep. Lack of sleep could also cause a bad temper. When people are unable to take a good rest, especially over days, this causes a snappy temperament.
9. Financial problems often make someone to be temperamental. People should try to be employed no matter how little the pay may be initially. Some agencies also reward volunteers, and it may be a good option to volunteer. Support services are available in some other cases to cater for the needy, for example the food banks and charity shops.
10. Marital problems. Marital turbulence causes emotional problems which could lead to emotional stress. A man or a woman in a turbulent or abusive marriage is usually temperamental. Aggrieved couples should discuss issues and try to be patient with one another. A period of separation may be needed.
11. Disability or illness. Many disabled people are not happy with their situation. The things they could do before are not been done easily and they need help which is not readily forthcoming. In environments when there are no lifts, for example and there are problems with accessing storey buildings for people on wheel chairs, there is a

tendency to a bad temper. Many disabled and sick people need to be treated with understanding and respect.

12. Academic problems. A bad temperament could be the result of academic problems, a bad temperament and changes in behaviour. Parents should be careful about how they react to teenagers and youth who all of a sudden exhibit deviant behaviour.

13. Overbearing responsibilities. When the day to day activities are too tasking and overbearing, the victims tend to be stressed. This is true for a nurse in a busy ward or a teacher with stubborn students. It could also be a particularly busy day, and tension and temperament are heightened. Human Resources Manager should take this into consideration.

14. Upbringing and life experiences. A person brought up in a hostile environment, or had a taunting experience in childhood and is used to a terrible lifestyle will always have a bad temper. People should try and put their past behind them as much as possible so that new things will begin to happen. Is 43:18 says remember ye not the former things nor consider the things of old, for I will do a new year's tomorrow

15. Unemployment. A person who is unemployed may experience frustration from time to time, especially when the have a need that is not easily met. The result is usually a bad temper, which sometimes lead to addictions or deviant behaviour.
16. Genetic issues. The human characteristics and behaviour are usually based on genetic factors. It is not uncommon to see people who inherited a bad temper. The father, was having temper problems, and was managed by a therapist. The son is beating his wife on a daily basis now, and yet one of the sons is always changing mood and unpredictable. A bad temper pattern in the family should be identified and solved.
17. Bereavement also can make people to demonstrate a short temper. A bereaved person must have been experiencing stress even before the moment of the loss of a beloved one. It is like a ripple effect when eventually the sad event occurs. People who are bereaved should be given maximum support emotionally.
18. Hunger is another factor that can make a person exercise a bad temper. When a person is hungry, they lose their patience and endurance. The result is a bad temper! This is especially true if it is a collective effect, like a leader who

has not paid the workers their salaries, or a teacher who has engaged the students for so long in class. They loose concentration. This is also true with children to a great extent, and it is generally said that a hungry man is an angry man.

19. Housing problems have been noted to provoke a bad temper. A person having accommodation problems is insecure and reacts to any slight provocation in as much as the problem persists. Quite a lot of people are facing accommodation problems.
20. Hormonal imbalances can affect the secretion of dopamine and serotonin which are neurotransmitters and have an effect on mood and irritability. This therefore could cause temper fluctuations.

The causes of stress need to be adequately addressed in order to live a healthy life, long life, have peace, and enjoy prosperity. As many as are going through the conditions highlighted above or have people around them going through same should act with caution. As soon as the problems are solved, a bad temperament can be put under check.

CHAPTER 3

REASONS WHY YOU NEED TO DEAL WITH YOUR TEMPER.

When you have a bad temper, and you don't deal with it, it could have devastating consequences on your life and destiny, having terrible effects on your health, quality of life, productivity, and even your length of days.

1. Going by the standard of the bible, James 4:17 states that to him that knoweth to do good and doeth it not, it is sin. A bad temper is unacceptable in the scriptures in Proverbs 14:17 – a quick tempered person does foolish things and the one who devises evil schemes is hated.
2. Every sin attracts a curse, and the bible says the way of the transgressor is hard (Proverbs 13:15-25), and there is no peace saith the LORD, unto the wicked (Isaiah 48:22). When you have a bad or snappy temper, you tend to lose out on many things and life becomes uneasy.
3. A very bad experience that you have with a bad temper is relationship problems. People find it extremely difficult to get along with you. Many of your friends are withdrawn

and uncooperative. A bad-tempered person often cannot work effectively as a member of a team.
4. Hinderance to opportunities. A snappy or bad temper will always deny you of opportunities. If there are opportunities for promotion in your place of work, for example that the role involves meeting with people, you wouldn't be a good fit for such a role. Any role that requires a lot of patience too would never be given to you.
5. Marital problems. When there are issues bothering on the temperament, it is difficult for a couple to adapt to one another and live peacefully. A temperamental couple will always disagree over small issues, and with intolerance.
6. Divorce rates are common in couples who cannot live peacefully together or tolerate one another. Incessant disagreement leads to resentment and ultimately divorce. Even if the issues of incompatibility are resolved and the temper is not addressed, there is every tendency for divorce, as a result of recurring issues.
7. Domestic violence. Intolerance and disagreements often lead to domestic violence. The marriage may become so bad that there is physical abuse on a regular basis. A person in a marriage like this often feels like been locked up in a prison. Most of these people regret their actions

later, at a time that it is rather late. Some lead to destruction of property and terrible losses financially.

8. Communication problems. In a workplace, in marriage, and in the society are not uncommon. It is very important to be able to communicate and relate to one another effectively in every society. It is also good for husband and wife at home to be able to communicate effectively and solve problems amicably. A temperamental person does not enjoy their career, and their marriage also. The result is that there is defeated purpose.

9. Mental health issues are common, when there is prolonged emotional stress due to a temperamental partner. This is not only true for the person who has temper issues, but the spouse also experiences same at the receiving end. Common mental health problems include depression, and anxiety.

10. Physical health issues. People who have cardiovascular disorders like hypertension, coronary artery disease, and arrhythmia. Someone with coronary artery disease may suffer from a heart attack and die. People with cardiovascular conditions should try as much as possible to manage stress from a toxic relationship, because it could be fatal.

11. Unanswered prayers may result from a bad temper. A bad temper is an umbrella of many different things like unforgiveness, anger, hatred, jealousy, and bitterness. A bad temper could be the only evidence the devil has against you. 1 Peter 3:7 encourages us to deal with our spouses according to knowledge, that our prayers be not hindered.
12. Problems in the workplace is not uncommon because it is difficult relating with somebody having a bath temper. They could disappear from work, or exhibit some strange behaviour. They could get very violent when there is an issue at work.
13. Loss of job. This is a possibility when the temperament is not controlled for a long time. The mistakes and the misdemeanours become too much and very obvious as it affects productivity at work. The employers will have no better option than to sack the worker.
14. A bad temperament creates a barrier between a person and the helpers. People who are willing to help will all of a sudden decide not to. This is because you are repulsive to people and possibly you are not a good teammate. It causes disfavour.

15. A bad-tempered person is always open to the spirit of error. When you are enraged or overtaken by your temper. The result is that you do things you intended not to do.
16. Error will always lead to offences. A bad temper can lead to legal issues at work or in marriage with devastating consequences. Most times, the crime of murder is usually due to a bad temper, as well as many other types of violence and misdemeanours. Some have been sentenced to prison terms just because they couldn't control their temper.
17. Bad dreams and nightmares. When you are temperamental, the calmness and serenity of spirit required to receive divine revelations cannot be achieved. God loves a broken
and a contrite heart and likes to talk to people that have these qualities. The calmer you are, the more you can relate with God the more you enjoy God.
18. When a person is temperamental without self control, then such a life is open and vulnerable to spiritual attacks. Demons move in freely and sponsor all types of affliction. Proverbs 25:28 says he that hath no rule (control) overfishing own spirit is like a city with broken down walls.

19. When a bad temper continues unchecked, it can lead to drug addiction. These people tend to escape frustration by taking drugs to mask their ugly experiences. Understanding it becomes worse.
20. Suicide often results from a bad temperament owing to an inability to be able to cope with life's challenges. We should take it upon us as members of the community to support people who are seen to be contemplating suicide.

CHAPTER 4

THE RELATIONSHIP BETWEEN SIN AND TEMPERAMENT.

Every bad deed causes provocation and a bad temperament. The Bible says to him that knoweth to do good and doeth it not, it is sin (James 4:17). Another view to this, means that temper arises from disobedience to God's word and a departure from every good purpose. The things you ought to do and you do not, or the things you ought not to do and you do them, fall under this category, in other words, the sin of omission, and the sin of commission, respectively.

1 John 3:4

Whosoever committeth sin transgresses also the law: for sin is the transgression of the law.

A bad temper arises because of the transgression against the law. Any violation of a law whether scriptural or man-made law could result in a bad temper. Violating laws in the workplace, at home, in the society, falling short of expectations are all causes of a bad temperament. We should try as much as possible to prevent a bad temper by obeying the laws and regulations at work, at home in the society and everywhere. Children of God should not enter into agreement or vows that they cannot fulfil, either with man or with God. Once we have entered into an agreement, or made a vow, we should make all possible efforts to fulfil the agreement or vow. Our ability to follow the commandments of God means peace. Ignoring this will lead to temper problems in our relationships and in every aspect of our lives.

There are things you have to do, that are your responsibility. Not doing it is sinful, and it could provoke a friend's, neighbour's or colleagues temper against you. There are responsibilities that you have to shoulder as a wife, or husband. There are responsibilities that you need to shoulder in your work place, there are responsibilities that you need to shoulder in church, and there are responsibilities that you need to shoulder in the society. If you fail to shoulder these responsibilities, then you are likely to face temper issues. Mind you, your inability to be able to meet up with these responsibilities could lead to annoyance, or temper issues.

Commission also could bring about temper issues. There are things that you keep doing, that you find difficult to stop. Some people are habitual latecomers, and no matter what they do, they still come late. In marriage, a dirty habit by one of the couples could be a continuous cause of temper and reaction to temper. There is not going to be peace, except this is stoped. There things we need to stop doing in our lives in order to have peace, healing, progress or other divine benefits.

Presumptuous sins. When committing presumptuous sins, you presume that everything is okay, even in spite of knowing or feeling that it is not right. David knew that sleeping with Uriah's wife was sinful, but he went on to commit the sin however. When you borrow something and use it without the consent of the owner, it is a presumptuous sin as well. Most of the sexual sins of adultery or fornication are presumptuous, but you still keep feeling that all is okay until you commit the sin.

A besetting sin is a sin that you are likely to commit because it is an area of weakness that you find very difficult to avoid. There is every temptation to commit this sin because of your weakness for it. Some people are naturally greedy that they find it difficult to look away from left over food. There are people who are also terribly addicted to alcohol that they find it extremely difficult to quit.

Hebrews 12:1

Wherefore seeing we also are compassed about with so great a cloud of witnesses, let us lay aside every weight, and the sin which doth so easily beset us, and let us run with patience the race that is set before us,

These are sins that you easily fall into, and are easy for you to commit. Besetting sins include laziness, pride or stubbornness, arrogance. All these could easily lead to temper issues.

CHAPTER 5

TURNING AWAY WRATH

In the chapter above, we have seen that our sins could provoke another people's anger against us. What then can we do to minimise the wrath of people against us, thereby bringing provocation or temperament to a halt. Overall, the human temperament is like a mirror. When your temperament is aggravated within you, it works against you. When other people are provoked against you, it works against you as well. How do we then minimise provocation of temperament against us?

1. Surrender to Jesus Christ, by confessing him as your Lord and saviour if you have not yet done so.
2. Sin will provoke anger against you. The best approach is to run away from every appearance of sin. Say no to temptation.
3. Learn to overlook certain things which will reduce your peace and joy. The Bible says that No man that warreth entangleth himself with the affairs of this life; that he may please him who hath chosen him to be a soldier. (2 Timothy 2:4).

4. Learn to reconcile and talk things over. James 5:16 advises us to confess our sins to one another that we might be healed (from a bad temper and possibly sickness).
5. There are people who are repulsive and bitter. Learn to keep a distance from them, lest they make you do what you don't want to do. People like that always make you to be bitter and upset.
6. Speak less and listen more. The more you speak the more likely are you to provoke someone. When you speak less, you are less likely to provoke people. As you listen more, you tend to het a clearer understanding of people, and how to relate with them without temper issues.
7. Learn to say sorry! When someone is really aggrieved and bitter, learn to tell them sorry. Learning to say sorry can turn away wrath as it is written in Proverbs 15:1 that a soft answer turneth away wrath: but grievous words stir up anger.
8. Learn to set boundaries for others and for yourself. Once you meet a person, you need to let them know what you don't like, as this creates a boundary between you and them. Also try and observe or ask them what they don't like. In some work places, the boundaries have been set already. In certain places of work, you know it is not right

to discuss with someone during work, or enter into their cubicle to take something.

9. Learn to forgive. We all are not perfect and are bound to offend one another. If that is the case then, we are always bound to offend one another. However, for peace to reign we need to forgive one another. Forgiveness is an attribute of the strong, and this is Godly, and wise in every situation.

10. Humility. This is very important in our relationship with others and is quite beneficial in turning away wrath. Humility simply is turning away from pride and arrogance. Humility involves a person's meekness, obedience to God's word, respect to yourself, respect to others, submission, and modesty.

CHAPTER 6

THE HUMAN TEMPER AND LIFE'S JOURNEY.

The life of man is a journey, and in this journey, he faces a lot of ups and downs that tend to influence our temperament and shake our existence in many ways. However, if we can tame our temper, then we can be able to navigate through the bus stops of life with ease. We are also able to relate with people for optimal benefits. Life is good if we are able to manage our temperament and respond with the knowledge and love of God to the feelings and temperament of others.

Let us see what affects the temper of man from cradle to grave.

Neonates.

Neonates react to many things thus affecting their temper.

One of the most common is when their diapers are wet, or they are feeling uncomfortable like heat or itches. Babies cannot talk, and it is therefore always necessary to try to find out why they are crying. They demonstrate a bad temper by crying and kicking. Even when you sing lullabies and pacify them, they continue kicking and crying, sometimes. Crying and kicking are usually the most common ways by which neonates display anger.

Another factor that may heighten the temper of a neonate is hunger. They tend to be very jittery when they are hungry. When you give them a shower and food, and they are still temperamental, then you think about fatigue or sickness.

A sick baby in addition to crying may have an increased body temperature, especially when they are growing the premolars and molar teeth. Some babies tend to be temperamental when they are constipated. When they are in pain, or need attention, they equally react with a heightened temper.

Children.

When children are misunderstood, then tend to be temperamental and jittery. That is why you should be patient and try to understand them. Another thing is that children love to be temperamental when they don't have an opportunity to play. Every child needs to play singly with their toys, or collectively with friends, to boost their mental health, and alertness.

Many adults like to play with children in the most absurd way, making joking and making mockery of them most times, especially when they have broken teeth, bed wet or their performance in school is not so encouraging. These occurrences are quite normal and should not be a cause for provoking children to wrath. Parents should understand whenever such occurs. Tiredness, especially after coming back from school and are very hungry, could make them temperamental. Frustration in carrying out a task at home or at school is a cause of heightened temper in children. They feel scared, for example at the time you want to give them an injection, or you tell them that a wild animal is coming to attack them.

Teenagers.

We need a lot of wisdom to handle temperament in teenagers, or temperamental teenagers. Peer pressure often makes a teenager demonstrate a bad temperament. The relationships they have in school can have a great toll on their temperament. Academic pressure can also affect their temperament if they are having difficulty at school. A bad teacher or inappropriate learning materials could contribute to this.

We should learn to counsel them and solve their academic problems so that they can be their best academically. A lot of hormonal changes are taking place in their bodies which make them agitated, excited or sometimes confused. They are bubbling with energy and may often misapply this energy to perform wrong and regretful tasks, leading to a bad temper. For example, a teenager went on an expedition and falls, or gets bitten by a dog. They regret their actions and het temperamental and jittery.

A lot of teenagers are struggling with identity problems. A teenager is developing, and he or she notices changes in the body. They now suddenly develop pubic hair, armpit hair, and males have a thicker voice. The females have breasts and enlarged hips, and all these make them sometimes to feel that they can do anything that a full-grown adult can do, or confused as to what to do sometimes, often to their own dismay and frustration. This happens the more, if they do not have the right parental advice and intervention which makes them more confused from a dominant peer pressure.

Parents should treat teenagers as friends, and be willing to come low to their level in order to be able to carry them along, ang gain their trust on confidential issues. Be willing to tell the females how to take care of their menstrual periods, and how to be hygienic. Let them know it is perfectly normal. Be open to satisfy their curiosities, and avoid frustration and heightened temper, which may lead to drug abuse. Parents should always be there for our beloved teenagers.

Most times, when you are unable to help them, they may experience self esteem issues. The thinking of a teenager is much more different to that of a child. A child does not really care about many things around them, if they can have good food and sleep well. A teenager is now conscious about their new looks, and how they compare with friends. They are also conscious about their academic performance in relation to their friends. A teenager who has a friend with affluent parents could try to compare themselves with their affluent friends, and think about their future and prospects.

All these may lead to inferiority complex and self esteem issues with terrible temper issues on a daily basis. They continue to ask themselves how they can tackle these self esteem issues, and if this cannot be resolved, it leads to aggravated temper, which may be the cause of deviant behaviour in some teenagers. This unfortunately is very common in teenagers if not properly addressed.

In order to resolve this, you need to be open to communication with these teenagers. When you are open to communication as a parent, teacher, or close person, they would be able to tell you more and increase their trust and confidence in you. With this advantage, you can come in to encourage them on a continuous basis and practice positive reinforcement. In positive reinforcement, you praise and sometimes reward a desired behaviour. If you are willing to reinforce good looks as a means to make them dress neatly and appropriately all the time, then you give him/her each time they dress very well, a compliment, and probably give some material things, or take them on an outing to a place they love.

Rejection problems are common in teenagers, first in the peer group, and from their family. The friends or peer group could reject and bully a teenager, because he does not conform to their norms and values. They may be vulgar and rascal because of their family backgrounds, whilst he is calm and humble, due to his upbringing, or personal preferences. This may make them to bully him. If he does not have a good rapport with his parents or guardians, and the right counsel, he will feel inferior, dissatisfied with life and temperamental. A lot of children, and adults are going through emotional stress, because they don't have someone that they can confide in, and share their problems with.

The family unit itself may reject a teenager owing to aggravated expectations that the teenager may possibly not be able to meet at that particular instance. Parents should be patient with teenagers, giving them time to develop and meet up with expectations academically and socially. Many teenagers tend to be rejected due to academic problems. The truth is that some catch up later in the secondary school years, and according to my late mother who was an educator, they are referred to as slow beginners. I was weak academically in Class 2 in the secondary school, but picked up in Class 4, and graduated with 7 distinctions and a credit at the School Certificate Examinations. My daughter who was weak academically all through the secondary school, got a scholarship for her 4-year program in the university, and came out with a first-class degree in Music. People pick up at different stages in life, so don't loose hope academically on any child.

The last issue that I will like to mention concerning temperament in teenagers is that they are overwhelmed by responsibilities. Even as they are struggling to find their bearing if they are children or adults, and trying to see how they can reconcile the new developmental changes physically, mentally and socially, with their abilities, parents saddle them with overwhelming responsibilities.

I was counselling a mother, one day, and her phone rang. The twelve-year-old daughter was calling from home and asking her, where she was, and that she should come home quickly, that she should come and take care of her children and that she was not the mother of the children and shouldn't be saddled with the responsibility of taking care of the children all day. She was very temperamental as she spat out those words from the bottom of her heart. Obviously, it was a weekend, and the mother had been away for several hours, leaving her a 12-year-old with the children. Let's be sensitive to their capabilities and not expect too much, in order to get the best from them and make them the best version that God wants them to be.

CHAPTER 7

TEMPERAMENT IN THE YOUTH.

One of the most challenging periods in life is during the youthful ages. By this I mean people between 20 years to 30 years old, and especially the ones that are yet to get married. It is a period of expectation, transition, and uncertainty maritally and financially. A bad temper could be very disastrous to prospective plans.

Youth are aware that the academic or career prospects are very important to their wellbeing and as a result are highly concerned about these. Majority of them are in higher institutions of learning and struggling to find their feet academically, socially or financially. Failure or disappointment in these areas could be very frustrating and cause a bad temperament. Those with good peer association and support tend to do well. Another factor, that helps is the family background. Family members that are willing to support could do a lot of good to the youth. It is a time as well that many of them may be distracted by youthful exuberance and a misplaced focus, and need close monitoring.

Family conflicts could be very disastrous during the youthful stage. These conflicts are a source of concern to the youth because of neglect, the enormous emotional stress, and sometimes physical and financial contribution for those who are employed. A youth who does not come from an affluent background could find it difficult to stand on his feet financially or otherwise. All these lead to stress and a bad temperament for as long as the situation lasts. Encouraging words do a lot of good at this stage.

Peer pressure could be another factor that may possibly lead to a bad temper. Youth tend to imitate one another, thereby trying to meet up with the status dictated by their peers. This is another cause of increased temper. Many of them resort to drug addiction when they cannot cope with the stress, which makes the situation more difficult.

The vulnerable social security system of the area or country that they belong to could also pose a big problem. When there is discrimination, poor healthcare delivery system, political problems, corruption, unemployment and many others, that could be frustrating. This could lead to a heightened tension and temper. This is why the youth should switch to the wisdom of God, in order to be able to tackle the problems. At this stage, the youth need counsellors. It is particularly rough when there is unemployment and the youth cannot provide for their basic needs. This can be very painful.

Identity issues could be very distressing and temper racking. Many youths get easily frustrated when they cannot fit into the society due to financial barriers. Cultural barriers could also contribute to a reduced self esteem in the youth, especially when it affects employment opportunities. The females are always preoccupied with looking good and fitting into their peer groups. Identity issues also could be academic in origin. In as much as a youth has a purpose, and a mission, and is working very hard to fulfil the mission, all will be well. The only problem is been carried away by the activities of the world, for no man that warreth entangleth himself with the affairs of this life (2 Timothy 2:4).

Relationship problems do contribute immensely as well to the heightening of the temperament in the youth. In a materialistic world, there is no true affection and true love goes to the highest bidder. The males because of economic recession are unwilling to marry early, with a large number of females that are unmarried. This is of major concern to the ladies who sometimes are single at 40 years old. A good number of them are also battling with divorce and other marriage problems.

Disappointment in relationships and finances can be very terrible. No one likes to be disappointed, after being stable and without a problem for so long, and suddenly disappointment comes, and every effort goes down the drain. Academically too, failing a test or exam repeatedly can be very disheartening, and can provoke your temperament. This can lead to substance abuse and even more complicated problems including suicidal tendencies.

Mental health issues are becoming very common in the youth and things like anxiety and depression are very common. The emotional burden in many quarters is so much, which is caused by unemployment and lack, mainly, and something needs to be done to attend to the numerous problems of the youth. Depending on several factors, like personal qualities, environment and support available, youth are able to adapt to different situations differently. A youth that cannot cope with stress will eventually develop mental health issues, and life may be very distressing and confusing. A youth that is able to adapt to life's stress will be above mental health issues, and have better outcomes in life. How do you deal with your youth, and how do you encourage or support them in their ambitions? Do they make use of various support services in the community?

Trauma or abuse is another thing that the youth are exposed to. Due to the global socioeconomic problems, there is a deviation from modest attitude and behaviour, leading to frustration and abuse in many quarters. An abused youth is emotionally traumatised and may be hostile to the society that has not met their expectations. Youth should be supported emotionally, so that they will not fall victims to a frustrated society. Association also determines your outcomes, and as such we should associate with the right people.

Embarrassment is feeling confused and ashamed. This is the exact situation that many youths find themselves. A lot of youth are trying and struggling to find their feet, academically, socially, career-wise, and financially. Most times, life is about trying, but when you try and fail, that is not the end. There is room for encouragement and demonstration of faith.

CHAPTER 8

CONQUERING BAD TEMPER AND ACHIEVING SUCCESS IN YOUR MARITAL JOURNEY.

Marriage is a like a journey in a boat, on the sea, and your temper is a horrible tempest, that can make that boat, called marriage to capsize, jeopardising the lives of people in the boat, consisting the husband, wife, children and significant others. Certainly, offences will come (Luke 17:1-4), but you need to control the tempest. The ability to do this will determine if you will get to the shore safely, and give glory to God. Mind you, this ability to control should be cultivated and sustained, because the storm may rock and capsize a boat, even when it is very close to the shore. It takes utmost care and I pray that God will give us the grace to follow and succeed at the end of our journey.

It is usually very blissful at the beginning of every marriage, say for the first one year, until reality begins to dawn on both couples. This is why courtship for up to a year is advised, before getting married eventually. It is not a good practice for intending couples to go to the altar without praying very well to seek the face of God, and knowing each other intimately during this period. Marriage is a lifelong contract and intending couples should not rush into marriage, else the storms of incompatibility will ravage their union and push then out of the marriage they love so much. If temper is not well controlled, it is not uncommon for a marriage of six months to hit the rocks. Contrary to this, if the couples are completely surrendered to God's will, and ready to do his will, they could live happily for the rest of their lives, with amazing blessings and testimonies to show for it.

Let us now explore the attitudes and behaviour that could affect the temperament of couples in marriage, and impact on the value of life, joy, blessings, health and longevity. We shall look at this for the first 20 years in marriage.

The first five years of marriage.

1. *Adjusting to new attitudes, behaviour, and routines* Joining and becoming one with a partner can be quite challenging sometimes, as you begin to learn how to adjust to attitudes, behaviour, and new routines. Previously as a lady, you could get up from bed whenever you wanted, but now you have to get up as early as 6am sometimes to

fix breakfast. This could raise a lady's temper. The husband needs to understand. In the first few weeks of pregnancy, a man who has not been used to waking up at night may have to do so now to take care of the pregnant wife or pack vomits. Some people don't like sleeping with the lights off, whilst some want it off. All these can contribute to an increased temper.

2. *Communication problems.* There are bound to be communication problems in newly married couples, because they are coming from different backgrounds and seem to misconstrue each other's opinion on occasions. Communication problems arise because of the differences in belief, orientation, and perception. For example, one of them may believe that house chores should be shared, but the other one may feel that certain roles should be the exclusive responsibility of a male or female. This can lead to temper issues.

3. *Cultural problems.* When there are differences in culture, and cultural beliefs, this can lead to temper issues. One partner may believe that the mother in law should visit regularly and stay for long periods with the daughter, but the other culture may not see it as necessary. Unmet expectations as a result of differences in culture can cause

temper issues, especially in the first few years of marriage. However, they adapt afterwards.

4. *Differences in upbringing.* There may be differences in upbringing which may lead to temper issues. A husband may believe that breakfast should be taken very early in the morning, but the wife may see it otherwise. The way the toilet is being used, or hygiene in the kitchen, may contribute to temper issues. However, as they grow together, they adapt to one another, as one of the parties invariably compromises.

5. *Financial load.* With marriage comes extra responsibilities in the first few years which they were not previously used to. Most times now, the when the husband or wife buys something, they buy for both of them, instead of one. They need to make allowance for their friends and relatives too. The expenses of care during pregnancy, and even a more elaborate accommodation, and a calculated change in status, all of which are quite normal, but requires more spending, and more sacrifice. Sometimes, the salary or income is grossly adequate, especially in cultures and religions that lay a greater expectation and responsibility on a man. This causes frustration and a bad

temper, and couples should be careful about the extent to which they adhere to expensive cultural practices.

6. *Shattered expectations.* There are things you expect when you get married. There are certain attitudinal and behavioural lapses which become obvious after marriage. You may discover that your wife or husband is dirty, or that your in-laws are becoming hostile. Spending preferences and habits could also be an issue, as well as work life balance. A partner may be too much of a workaholic, giving very little time for Intimacy in marriage. All these things will only surface after they get together and dialogue and sincere communication should be adopted to overcome this.

7. *Family dynamics.* The influence of parents and in-laws could really constitute a big problem especially in the first few years of marriage, for people that are too attached to their parents. Some husbands or wives sleep in their family houses more often, than spending time with their spouse, and keep discussing their family issues. They could also be tempted to commit a greater part of their resources to their siblings, rather than with their spouses and children. This impacts greatly on the family dynamics and may cause heightened temper, bitterness and disagreement.

8. *Bad conflict resolution.* When conflict resolution between couples seem to be partial, there will be heightened temper in the aggrieved or unfairly treated partner. Friends, families and religious leaders should be honest and fair in resolving conflicts between couples. This will not only lead to a bad temper, but could also lead to hatred amongst couples.
9. *Intimacy issues* could arise with a partner found wanting. A newly married person would like to spend time with the partner. This may not be possible due to a busy work schedule, family or social engagements. If there is no understanding, there will be temper problems which may affect cohesion in their marriage.
10. *External stressor*, like a partner working so far from home, and being caught up in traffic may get home and is very jittery. The workload in the place of work too could be terrible and make either of the couple aggressive or temperamental. Health problems too could lead to temper problems especially if it is psychological.
11. *Role changes* in the place of work could bring about temper problems, as well as at home. This is especially true if a partner has a long-term ailment. A partner who goes for night duties too may experience some negative

attitude from the partner once a while, or all the time. This why couples should be open to communication.

12. *Personal growth disappointments.* There are expectations of the man or woman as to personal development. Most new couples are anxious about the heights they want to reach in life and as a result of this they are disappointed if they don't achieve that on time, and are jittery. This can lead to temper issues.

CHAPTER 9

TEMPER IN THE SIXTH TO TENTH YEARS OF MARRIAGE.

Going forward from the fifth to tenth year of marriage, there are peculiar temper issues to be addressed. The marriage is evolving, and new things are showing up on the scene, sometimes shocking and frustrating, and sometimes very bright and encouraging. Research has shown that the majority of divorce cases occur within the sixth and tenth year of marriage. This is what we shall be looking at under this subheading.

1. *Communication problems*. Communication problems continue till the 5th to 10th year of marriage, even though the couples are now familiar with one another more than they used to be, but the communication problems are deeper and more complex. There are still times when there will be misconceptions, which will ultimately lead to temper issues. A great deal of understanding and patience is necessary at this time.
2. *There are unresolved conflicts* at this time of the couple's life, and there seems to be more familiarity, which breeds contempt, the result is that there are several unresolved

matters. Years 7-8 stand out as the years in marriage when the greatest rates of divorce occur. It is a time to be very careful about the management of temper. Things just degenerate.

3. *Life transitions*. The 5th to 10th years of marriage pose very challenging problems and transitions. There is always a barrier to cross and a battle to fight. The people that are not able to endure these transitions end up in divorce. These constant challenges lead to temper issues need to be patiently approached and the marriage protected.

4. *Parenting challenges*. There tends to be a diversity of views on parenting. If these diversities are not addressed prayerfully and patiently, there is conflict and temper issues in the marriage. Husband and wife should always be willing to come together, despite their preferences, to settle their differences.

5. *External stressor and situations*. The couple has developed more extensive personal relationships at work, and in the society at large. There is enormous external strain and stress on the relationship that could cause issues and increased temper. This may include misconceptions about issues, especially when they decide to resolve issues by taking advise from friends, instead of solving it together.

Two marriages cannot be the same, and so you cannot follow the advice of friends in a strict manner. Challenges with regards to career could also cause temper issues, likewise health issues. The strategy of winning together is excellent. Do things by proffering solutions together.

6. *Financial challenges.* As the marriage progresses, there are increasing needs and responsibility. The financial demands are increasingly more than it used to be, but the income is the same. This financial strain generates temper issues. There could also be unemployment and career challenges. The couple may also start dealing with debts because of increased responsibility. Couples should learn to support one another, not only financially but emotionally. Multiple streams of income should be sought, as expenditure are being reviewed arriving at meaningful options.

7. *Emotional Intimacy.* There could be problems with emotional Intimacy, and couples may tend to lose the initial burning of the fire of affection and emotions as it was initially. Often one partner feels cheated at times, and if care is not taken, the emotional connection is lost. Couples should sacrifice time for family cohesion.

8. *Relationship neglect* is real at this time, as most couples have seemingly had enough of one another, if they are not

in Christ. At this stage many tend to be emotionally detached or altogether abandon their relationships. Some spend more time with their parents, and at the end of the day, the children suffer. If care is not taken, the experience of the children at this time even as young as they are may leave lifelong negative effects on their destinies

9. *Infidelity issues.* It is at this stage that the devil may bring imaginations and thoughts to deceive you, as you come to some fake realisation. The devil may tell you that your husband is a poor man, and he may not give you the kind of life you anticipated. He would argue further in your thoughts, that enough of the suffering, and hardship. There might be a tendency to trying out other men or women, and trying out new dangerously dangerous experiments. The reality is that the strange man or woman, have nothing to offer you than to take advantage of you, sexually and materially. The wise option is to support your partner towards higher achievements. The devil may tell you that your wife is no longer beautiful or nut good in bed any longer. This leads to infidelity. However, there is no better replacement for your spouse, and there is no better fit. Infidelity in marriage is a terrible problem that could generate terrible temper issues.

10. *Priority changes* arise as couples advance in age, in career, and experience. This might not be the same for both couples as there are differences in life experience and things the couple's values. This discrepancy may lead to misunderstanding and temper issues. Couples should try and align their values with understanding and maturity. Communication will help couples balance and align their priorities.

CHAPTER 10

HANDLING TEMPER ISSUES IN THE ELEVENTH AND FIFTEENTH YEARS INTO MARRIAGE.

There is now a world of changes in preferences between the husband and the wife, due to age, physical changes, career changes and other factors.

1. *Stagnation.* It is not uncommon that at some point in time, a non-analytical couple mat be tempted to believe that they are stagnated and stuck, especially if there is increased financial responsibilities overwhelming upon the finances. Some couples compare themselves with other couples and this causes a heightened temper. The solution lies in coming together to review the situation and see what next needs to be done.
2. *Medical problems.* As age increases, there are health issues to contend against. There could be problems with the eyesight, high blood pressure, arthritis, or others which begin to show up, and may begin to be a source of concern to the couple. If not patient enough the extra care required by an infirm partner may be a source of frustration for couples who are not in faith. Husband and

wife at this stage should remember their marital vows, to love and to hold in health and sickness, for poorer and for richer. Temper problems cannot but arise, but your beliefs and perceptions will help a great deal.

3. *Midlife crisis.* This is a period in life, usually between the age of 40 – 60 years of age, that people begin to reflect on the accomplishments and achievements in life, evaluating same. They tend to reflect on their life mistakes and unmet expectations, and there are a lot of these. This brings about regret and frustration especially as regards their marriage, and career. This brings a heightened temperament. Instead of counting the frustrations why don't you just count your blessings and give God the glory. There is no life without some regrets, but you should not focus on them, as it multiplies your sorrow. The Bible says a broken spirit drieth the bones (Proverbs 17:22). Thinking about materials and riches aggressively pierces you with many sorrows (1 Timothy 6:10).

4. *The empty nest syndrome.* When the children begin to leave home for the first time, to school, to work, or for marriage, there is a sense of depression and loneliness that parents especially the mothers experience. This is especially so for single parents or parents that do not

share a cordial relationship. This can provoke the temper in the troubled parents.

5. *Career changes*. Career changes may be necessary due to health reasons, change in financial circumstances, monotony and boredom, or simply trying to achieve a life-work balance. Changing a career most times bring about instability, worries and frustration about exactly what the future holds. This can lead to a bad temper and depression. However, if you trust God and keep working hard, all will be well. It is only a matter of time.

6. Sexual Intimacy could lead to a bad temper at this time, as one of the couples tend to desire it more than the other. The man may start having signs of erectile dysfunction whilst the wife desires more sexual intimacy. On the other hand, the man may desire a closer sexual Intimacy, whilst the wife is always preoccupied with the welfare of the children and meeting their needs. Menopause may also be taking it's toll on the woman. These issues may cause a heightened temperament and aggression.

7. Erosion of trust could also build up out of several disappointments down memory lane. People tend to get frustrated because of this and are cautious with relationships whilst sometimes being unnecessarily bitter

and temperamental. The Bible tells us in Colossians 3:13 to be forbearance and forgiving, and this should be the right attitude.

8. Lifestyle differences between husband and wife could develop leading to a heightened temperament. Lifestyle differences between husband and wife could be due to differences in health challenges, differences in career responsibilities, for example, one of the partners travel a lot, or stays late at work, while the other is lonely at home. Family influence, social influence and personal preference with time could lead to lifestyle changes and a heightened temperament. Husband and wife should come together and discuss the way out. couples also need to be considerate creating more time at home for companionship.

CHAPTER 11

THE IMPACT OF A BAD TEMPER IN THE WORKPLACE AND PRODUCTIVITY.

In the workplace a bad temper could have devastating effects on productivity and revenue generation. It could also have an effect in such a way that works contrary to the corporate image of the organisation. This is why it becomes very important for the leadership in the organisation to formulate policies aimed at managing bad temperaments in the workplace.

The truth is that leaders in the organisation, colleagues, and subordinates all have a role to play with regards to the management of temper in the workplace as we are going to explain in the workplace one-by-one in the following paragraphs.

How do we manage temperament in bosses?

Micromanagement. There are bosses in the workplace that like to micromanage every activity of the subordinates thereby making them temperamental. Excessive attention and comments on the work of a subordinate could be counterproductive instead of increasing production. It has to be done with love.

For a queer boss, communication is key so that you try to give them all the details necessary to make them happy and to gain their confidence. When you do this, it will reduce drastically every tendency by your boss to micromanage. This will give you more autonomy and happiness.

Delays in decision making could be another mistake in a boss that could trigger a bad temperament. There are bosses that are naturally slow in decision making when you expected them to be quicker. In this case you may support in decision making where possible. This does not however mean that you dictate the pace but only to support the process. This can go a long way to douse temperaments.

A critical boss is another factor that could affect your temperaments. This type of boss will always criticise whatever you do instead of correcting you in love. "I'm telling you why the things you have done are not good enough". Such a leader could really get you upset and increase your temperaments so that work might not be interesting. You need to try as much as possible to be patient had to be teachable with such bosses. While you do this, you'll be able to cope with a critical boss.

Delays in payments or salaries, bonuses, and entitlement can make a worker to be temperamental. if the delay comes occasionally it might be understood as an error. However, if the delay is frequent in your payments and without any reasonable reason you will witness many months of payments in arrears which is not good for you, and in such a case, you may need to consider finding a new job.

Favouritism in the workplace another factor that could bring about heightened temperaments and discouragements in the place of work. Some bosses show favouritism based on geographical status, or for economic reasons. Every leader should try as much as possible to avoid favouritism or avoid being partial. Such actions should be reported to the appropriate quarters, all sorted out through consultation with the leader. Sometimes you may not need to take any drastic action be cause the issue will resolve naturally. One major reason for working is because of your salaries and wages. In as much as you can get this, then you should try an be patient till the appointed time.

Managing issues with colleagues.

Competitive colleagues can be a big problem a big problem Because of unhealthy rivalry. A competitive colleague is full of all manners of repulsive behaviour and provocation which can heighten a person's temper. One thing you can do is to collaborate wisely with them and acknowledge their contributions.

A negative colleague is another type of colleague that can provoke your temperaments. They will always never see anything positive but negative things. They always have a reason why something should not work, and may upset your temper considerably because of their negativity. When you work with such people you need a lot of positive reinforcements, in which you encourage an acknowledge the positive contributions, and you dwell more on solutions to problems and dwell less on negativity.

An unreliable colleague is another type of colleague that heightens your temper in the workplace. They find it difficult to achieve progress alone and this can be very annoying. When it happens this way what you need to do is that you need to set goals, deadlines and priorities. This will go a long way in making them to follow the set goals and timeframes whilst being reliable.

A chauvinistic colleague is another type of colleague that can make you angry an upset your temper if you are not careful. When dealing with the chauvinistic colleague you need to maintain calmness and professionalism, otherwise they might make you to misbehave. The second thing is for you to set boundaries between you and them, and make sure they recognise and follow the set boundaries. Documents every impolite activity in case you may need to present it before the human resources department. Consider talking it over with them, and with your human resources manager. let them know that you are not happy with such an attitude, or behaviour as the case may be.

Managing temperament in the subordinates.

Subordinates at work could be fighting your temper and you need to be able to control the situation for maximum professionalism and productivity. Controlling your temperament also has benefits on your health.

A passive subordinate is the first type of subordinate you need to deal with that can affect your temperament. This type of subordinate does not take initiatives of their own. They are hardly seen to make meaningful contributions. In this case, you need to clearly define their roles, and set timelines, making sure you monitor them, just as you motivate them.

A lazy subordinate can also upset your temper, because they tend not to demonstrate reasonable productivity. Set targets for people like that, and supervise them making sure the targets are met. It is also desirable to motivate them and encourage them.

Unintelligent subordinates could also heighten your temperament with their decisions, actions, and quality of service. People like this may need further training, emphasising on weak areas. They also need supervised hands-on experience. Patience is needed to bring out the best in such colleagues.

Overconfident subordinates could not only fall into error, but may tend to be stubborn as well. This may provoke a bad temper from people around them in the workplace. People like this need to be provided with clear guidelines and constructive comments. They should be held responsible for excesses to serve as a deterrent some other times.

Subordinates resistant to change are another group of workers that could transmit a negative charisma and provoke peoples' temperaments in the workplace. They are unwilling to learn, and resist new innovations and could be rude. People like this would benefit from explicit communication, explaining to them why it is important to embrace change, under the circumstances.

Incorrigible subordinates will never take to corrections, and may be rebellious to constituted authority. The best approach is to make sure that they are liable to every error, to the extent of paying for any financial consequences.

Managing self temperament.

As a worker in the workplace, whether working as a boss, co-worker with a group, or subordinate. A worker should be able to manage his or her temperament for the reason of good productivity, their health and professionalism. The following steps are helpful in controlling your temperament, as a person:

Self-awareness. Every man should find out what their weaknesses are in the workplace. It is good to note which things provoke your temperament, how, when and where. When you know these, you may want to avoid getting temperamental.

Stress management. There are steps you need to take in managing stress including relaxation, massage, meditation, exercise therapy, diet control, sleep adequately, hobbies, and time management. One of the stated methods or a combination of them can work wonders.

Effective communication is another method of self management of your temper. Most times, frustration and a bad temper go hand in hand. A good strategy for effective communication between you and other members of staff will go a long way in dissipating a negative temperament. The Bible says, can two walk together except they be agreed (Amos 3:3).

A good problem-solving approach. When there is misunderstanding and a heightened temperament, a good problem-solving approach can be very helpful. The lapses in problem solving may be due to inadequate knowledge, sequence of operations, timing, or other factors. It is necessary to sit down as a team and explore what the problem may be with a view to solving it. When a good problem-solving approach is adopted, then the problem of the temperament can be easily solved.

Expert advise could also be of tremendous help, and the advice of a counsellor or expert can be of immense benefits. This may be internal or external, and a consultant could be invited to review the circumstances and proffer solutions. A very important approach to solving problems in life is through counselling, but many people under-rate the importance of counsel in solving problems.

Ten scriptures that highlight the importance of counselling and seeking wisdom:

1. Proverbs 11:14 "Where there is no guidance, a people fail, but in an abundance of counsellors there is safety."
2. Proverbs 15:22: "Without counsel plans fail, but with many advisers they succeed."
3. Proverbs 19:20 "Listen to advice and accept instruction, that you may gain wisdom in the future."
4. Proverbs 20:18: "Plans are established by counsel; by wise guidance wage war."
5. Proverbs 24:6: "For by wise guidance you can wage your war, and in abundance of counsellors there is victory."

6. Psalm 1:1: "Blessed is the man who walks not in the counsel of the wicked, nor stands in the way of sinners, nor sits in the seat of scoffers."
7. James 1:5: "If any of you lacks wisdom, let him ask of God, who gives to all liberally and without reproach, and it will be given to him."
8. Proverbs 12:15: "The way of a fool is right in his own eyes, but a wise man listens to advice."
9. Proverbs 13:10: "By insolence comes nothing but strife, but with those who take advice is wisdom."
10. Ecclesiastes 4:13 "Better was a poor and wise youth than an old and foolish king who no longer knew how to take advice."

Prayer and fasting are ways of seeking counsel from the Lord, and it is the best counsel you can get in order to solve problems. However, it may take a lot of time, but you have to be patient. Fasting can be in different forms, and you could break your fast in the afternoon or evening, for several days until you get a reply. God will surely give you an "answer of peace" (Genesis 41:16), if you tarry long enough. Some options of fast available are a white fast, whereby you do not eat anything made with oil, salt, sugar, pepper, meat or fish. Or a fruit fast, whereby you take only fruits during your fast. It is important to have a note where you record your dreams, and revelations. An interpreter (Job 33:23) may be needed to interpret your dreams, if they are dark speeches, or even similitudes (Numbers 12:8).

CHAPTER 12

THE IMPACT OF TEMPERAMENT ON PHYSICAL AND MENTAL HEALTH

Temperament builds and determines your personality, your behaviour and outcomes in life. The temperament is inborn and determines how you respond to environmental changes around you, and even those things around you. It determines how you move with the tides of life. Our outcomes in life consist not only in what happens to us, but largely upon how we respond to the things that happen to us.

A profound understanding of the individual's temperament will not only help in predicting their outcomes in life, but also can help in developing strategies aimed at improving health and overall wellbeing.

There are four main types of temperaments observed in humans, with each having their strengths and weaknesses, while also giving us an understanding about how people behave the way they do. This means that broadly, all human beings follow after four main behavioural and personality traits. This will help our dealing with people, enhancing effective communication, and because of the understanding gained, we can enhance our health and wellbeing, as well as theirs. It is also a boost for professional relationships and overall productivity as has been mentioned earlier on.

It is good to note that these individual temperaments could be altered and managed for individual benefits, especially as it affects the health of individuals and populations. There tends to be an overlap in the characteristics associated with each personality trait, such as culture, upbringing, exposure, level of education, and other factors tend to influence the temperament.

The four major types of temperament are; sanguine, cholera, melancholic, and phlegmatic.

Sanguine personality.

The sanguine personality is a lively, out-going, adventurous, fun-loving, sociable, and care-free person. He is also optimistic, buoyant and romantic. They move with all, and can tolerate all sorts of people. They have zero tolerance for boredom and will always seek variety and have a flair for entertainment, arts and communication. They are also very creative. Professionally, they do well in jobs related to these. They are highly impulsive and quick to conclude and decide, without much thinking.

Let's see how these characteristics affect how they feel in sickness, how likely are they to seek help, how they comply with prescriptions and guidelines, as well as what types of diseases that are likely to be predominant with this type of temperament.

The health vulnerabilities of a sanguine personality

A sanguine personality is prone to infectious diseases, due to the fact that they are social butterflies that like meeting people, and are out going. This may include flu, veneral diseases, sore throat, and other communicable diseases. There is also a tendency to drug addiction and substance abuse, due to their fun-loving nature.

A sanguine personality could be reckless and adventurous, making then prone to domestic accidents as well as road traffic accidents. Digestive problems may be common due to a reckless care-free life and irregular eating patterns.

A sanguine personality is free minded and is dynamic. This makes them to be able to put their blood pressure and the problem of cardiovascular disease under check, as well as stress related conditions like depression and anxiety. His mental health holds great prospects due to his optimistic and sociable life.

A sanguine may be very busy with activities and might not initially seek help when they are sick. He gets sociable in the hospital setting and is well known. He can wangle his way through to get anything that he wants. They are likely to cooperate with doctors and nurses in taking their medication. They are more likely to cooperate with hospital procedures that are quick, in as much as they have understood the procedure and benefits. Even after leaving hospital, has friends that still communicate regularly with them. It is possible that at the beginning of their sickness and upon admission in the hospital, or isolation at home, they feel very uncomfortable because they are the outgoing and sociable type.

A sanguine individual is a good candidate for faith-based healing, because of their liberal nature and free mindedness.

Choleric personality.

A person with a choleric personality is rather goal oriented, and likes to be analytical and logical. They are critics, and will normally think twice before doing things. They usually do not like to be too friendly or show companionship. They probably will not like to be in the company of friends, chatting away, but rather like to be engaged with more involving complex and troublesome situations. They do not associate with everyone, but rather people that belong to the same professional circles.

Cholerics may not be too romantic, though on the surface they may appear to be. They will always take some time to prioritise their professional duties. Cholerics do well in leadership, management, engineering, programming, business, statistics and other numerate and analytical disciplines.

Let's see how these characteristics affect how they feel in sickness, how likely are they to seek help, how they comply with prescriptions and guidelines, as well as what types of diseases and health downsides that are likely to be predominant with this type of temperament.

The health vulnerabilities of a choleric personality

The serious mindedness and goal-oriented life of a choleric individual, tends to put them through stress, with a tendency for high blood pressure and cardiovascular disorders. A choleric may also have symptoms pertaining to anxiety disorders, tension headaches, and migraines. A choleric with a tendency to heart attack, or with a family history of such, needs to take life easy, especially as they grow older.

An analytical lifestyle may make a choleric to begin to imagine and focus on minor ailments. Gastrointestinal problems are likely like gastritis, gastric and duodenal ulcers, and similar diseases. A tendency to overwork may lead to emotional fatigue, muscle fatigue, burnout and others.

A choleric will most likely be angry to be abased and seeing themselves subject to nurses and doctors instead of the usual leader's lifestyle and assertiveness. They are not able to tolerate long stays in the hospital, and during his stay, he's always focused on his duties, though they like to be in control, and may be attracted to solving problems in the hospital environment. A choleric may also be assertive to the nurses, trying to tell them what they should do. They are likely to comply with medication regimen. A choleric may be sceptical, when it comes to co-operating with hospital procedures, unless they are able to verify a need for them, because of their analytical nature, and a penchant for details.

Melancholic personality.

A melancholic personality is very creative, and sensitive to happenings within and without, but are introverts. They could bottle their emotions, and put on a facade. Nothing is ever good enough as their standards are very high. They tend to criticise and are pessimistic. They rather tend to work and play alone in their own little space. They are happy that way! When you understand this, you let them be. They are very thorough with a flair for precision and accuracy.

Melancholic people love traditions and culture. Their lives are coloured by cultural norms, sanctions, and values. They love their families and friends, but contrary to the sanguine are not outgoing, adventurous, fun loving and the likes. They tend to shy away from such dispositions. Someone with a melancholic personality will always eat foods from their indigenous countries while in another country and tend to put on clothing indigenous to their countries. They are highly conservative about their traditions and culture and may not like to leave their home lands or get married to a foreigner. Melancholic are however romantic people, hiding in their shell with their partner.

Melancholic are best suited for occupations in management, accounting, social work or administration, and similar disciplines.

Let's see how these characteristics affect how they feel in sickness, how likely are they to seek help, how they comply with prescriptions and guidelines, as well as what types of diseases and health downsides that are likely to be predominant with this type of temperament.

The health vulnerabilities of a melancholic personality.

A melancholic personality is highly sensitive to happenings within him or his environment and as such is prone to depression, whenever he is disappointed, or prone to anxiety, if he is unable to get what he wants on time. Furthermore, because he is prone to always being a perfectionist, obsessive compulsive disorder may be likely. Loss of memory is also possible due to an overloading of the brain with tasks, as well as being jittery at times.

Chronic stress can weaken the immune system, this is another problem that is likely in people who are melancholic. Psychosomatic pain could be common in a melancholic person because of high stress levels and emotional sensitivity. Sleeplessness or insomnia may be common in a person who is melancholic, because they are perfectionists and won't likely sleep until they have a task accomplished.

A person with a melancholic temperament is pessimistic and could be worried about their health, trying to figure out the worst possibility about what can happen. The symptoms may be exaggerated because of this. They are likely to seek help immediately, after a diligent search and they are convinced about the urgency of a need for therapy. They tend to be meticulous in taking medications and are very likely to comply, especially in tested and trusted procedures. Melancholic will definitely yield to logical procedures in the hospital.

Usually because of the critical and pessimistic nature, they couldn't be good candidates for spiritual care.

Phlegmatic personality.

Someone with a phlegmatic personality is usually calm, self-controlled, not easily provoked, easy going, patient and tolerant.

He is slow to get angry, and is accommodating because they fear conflicts. Phlegmatic personalities tend to be guilty and blame themselves usually when things go wrong in a relationship. They maintain commitments and will not like to come late if they have an appointment with you. They will always deliver when they promise you something. Phlegmatic personalities are introverts and will most often than not like to be on their own.

Phlegmatic people in a team tend to seek your opinion in making decisions, rather than be over-riding. A phlegmatic person will most likely not want to attend parties frequently. Phlegmatic people may be romantic, but it takes some time to get connected in matters of the heart. Thus, is the most sensitive of all personality types.

Phlegmatic people are good as administrative secretaries, book keeping and finance, clerical duties, nurses, personnel officers conflict managers, diplomats, doctors, surgeons, architects, and other professions that require a lot of patience.

Let's see how these characteristics affect how they feel in sickness, how likely are they to seek help, how they comply with prescriptions and guidelines, as well as what types of diseases and health downsides that are likely to be predominant with this type of temperament.

The health vulnerabilities of phlegmatic personalities.

A tendency towards a sedentary disposition could lead to obesity, and other disorder arising from lack of physical exercise. Muscle weakness, impaired cardiovascular and respiratory function, joint stiffness, high cholesterol, reduced insulin production and impaired blood glucose level control especially in people with type 2 diabetes. Erectile dysfunction arthritis, and cognitive dysfunction are very likely.

Depression results if they are unable to achieve their goals. The introverted nature often prevents the phlegmatic person from exercising, but rather they prefer to stay indoors, or glued to their work. Muscle disorders, muscle weakness, joint pain, and reduced joint movement could be present especially as they grow older. A lack of adequate physical exercise can also predispose to cardiovascular problems, especially in people that have a family history of cardiovascular diseases, or in elderly patients.

Phlegmatic persons are often withdrawn, or neutral about their sickness, maintaining a quiet and unperturbed attitude. They are gentle and may not seek help immediately because of their gentle and simple nature. However, if they are prompted, they conform immediately. They comply with medications and hospital procedures that are very simple and hassles free, especially after you have courteously explained to them.

A phlegmatic individual is a good candidate for faith-based healing, because they are obedient to a fault in carrying out instructions.

CHAPTER 13

STRESS MANAGEMENT

Stress is a major contributing factor to the generation and demonstration of a negative temperament. Everyday, we go through situations that stretch us beyond our limits at work, at home, in the community or at play, known and unknown. Our ability to be able to cope with these stressors impact to a great extent, the quality of life, and how long subsequently we are able to live in life. Stress management is very important and is something everyone should be interested in.

What is stress?

Stress can be defined as bodily or mental exertion caused by physical or mental stressors, and making the human body and brain to exceed it's physiological and psychological limits.

Stress and its impact.

Stress makes life very uncomfortable and miserable, with anxiety, depression, and other emotional issues. When stress is overwhelming, it is difficult to concentrate and relax. There is confusion and inability to perform our daily tasks satisfactorily. There is pain and tiredness, irritability, headaches, a troubled spirit and disturbed sleep. There is a reduction or exaggeration of appetite. People with underlying health conditions could experience a worsening, especially the mental health disorders. It would be obvious that urgent healthcare may become necessary, but some erroneously may tend to take alcohol, cigarettes, or marijuana and others, which have negative consequences on their health and healing.

What are common approaches to stress management?

Have a pet

Having a pet like a dog, a cat, a bird or monkey is a good thing. Caring for these animals can be really something that brings happiness and relaxation. The gestures of animals like dogs or monkeys especially can be really funny, and interesting. They make a good company when you are stressed emotionally.

Sleep

A lot of sleep is important in order to manage stress, be it of emotional or physical origin. Sleep is also good when someone is recovering from illness, as it helps the body to repair. It is desirable to have at least about 8 hours of sleep on a daily basis.

Comedy

This is very good for relieving stress too, and you can enjoy it on the television, at the theatre, or on the YouTube, as well as in day to day living and activities.

Aromatherapy

This involves using scents and fragrances to bring relaxation and stress relief. There are certain fragrances and incenses that have a pleasant sensation on the olfactory system, and brings relief from stress. It could be used in the bedroom, or in the car. Fragrances could also be used in the sitting room and other rooms within your house.

Spend time with people you love

Spending time with people you love can really bring about relaxation. They have a good effect on your soul, and there are people like that in everyone's life. Stay away from negative and toxic people that add to your stress.

Spa

Find something you enjoy doing e.g. cooking, swimming, drawing, cake dressing, playing an instrument of music, can be very pleasant to the soul, and bring about relief from stress. Finding time to do this over a long period can really be fulfilling.

Go on a drive.

Driving could be a nice experience and stress relieving in several ways. Some people enjoy driving in the company of people they love, visiting parks or other places of interest. Some just prefer to drive on a long journey, listening to soft music with a sunshade on, and viewing the beauty of the countryside.

Meditation.

Meditation is a practice that has existed for thousands of years. Christian meditation is carried out by finding a cool place to relax, and make sure you are positioned well. Then you may close your eyes and switch off the lights. Begin to think about the word of God that relates to your problems, and ask questions within you that, why, when, what, where, and how that revolves around your question. Be still for a while, as you listen for a word (Psalm 4:4). When you are still, you make a search in the spirit, for the spirit of man is the candle of the Lord (Proverbs 20:27). It is beneficial to write on a piece of paper, anything, that is revealed to you.

Spend time with a therapist.

A therapist is a professional, and qualified person who is able to engage you in a discussion, and is very quick at discovering reasons, why certain things are happening. They are also in a good position to proffer long lasting solutions to your problems. Usually, a person could access a therapist through their general practitioners or by self referral in England and Wales. It is also possible to have a face-to-face or online session.

Exercises.

These are valuable and rank among the best methods of relieving stress. However, based on your health status, certain exercises may be more appropriate for you, and exercise testing and prescription may be relevant, depending on your circumstances. Aerobic exercises are usually highly tolerable, but you should watch out for symptoms like tiredness or dizziness, when you are undergoing exercise, and these are indicators that you need to stop temporarily or permanently for the day.

Massage.

Massage or soft tissue manipulation also helps in relieving stress. There are different types of massage techniques. There is effleurage, or relaxation massage, which involves a gentle manipulation of the skin and muscles with a relaxing effect on the nerve endings. Oil or powder may be applied to the surface of the body in order to have a smooth manipulation. The bed or couch used, the tilt of it, and the nature of the mattress would all have an impact on the overall feeling. Aromatherapy could be combined with massage for an enhanced effect.

Analyse and set boundaries

Music and dance. Music and dance could also have a great impact upon your ability to have a relaxed and stress-free life. Listening to music can be a good choice for taking off stress, after work hours. Depending on the kind of lyrics, beats, rhythm, or instruments that you enjoy listening to. It is very common for music with lyrics that address your challenges in a soothing manner to bring about relaxation. Some also enjoy lyrics in a particular language, which may not even be their language. It is not uncommon sometimes for a husband to want to listen to music in the wife's language, when they don't speak the same language. The love and affection between husband and wife then has musical dimensions. Music with a slow tempo and continuous nature with light percussion and simple rhythm are very appropriate. Classical music, and instrumental jazz are also very suitable. Gospel music carries inspirational and motivational lyrics and are as such very appropriate for stress management. Certain sounds like a rushing water, winds, or even the sounds of animals like birds, can be very pleasant to the ears and to the soul, and are available on YouTube.

Writing.

The human brain is jam-packed with different types of stuff from day-to-day experience, and it could bring some form of stress, if you can't express or let out some of these ideas. It is so pleasant and fulfilling to a sanguine personality for example, as well as a choleric, to share their ideas, through a debate, speaking with people, or in a written form. Written stuff could be in form of reports, or fiction or non-fiction books. It is always a happy feeling if you are able to share your experience with other people.

Visiting places of interest.

A visit to a zoo, or museum, can be really nice, when you are not in the best of moods, and are stressed up. However, activities in places like this should be optimal, so that it doesn't bring much more stress at the end of the day. Sometimes, when you are in the company of a friend and are chatting all the way, you may not feel much stress, compared to when you go alone.

Cinema.

There are different cinema houses in many cities around the world, that show different kinds of content. We all have something that interest us. Some may have a flair for romantic films, whilst others have an interest in documentaries, and others may take an interest in comedy. At any particular point in time, you would know intuitively what best suits you, and can calm you.

Social media

The social media, like Facebook, YouTube, Instagram, WhatsApp to mention a few, all have engaging content that could take away stress. This includes news, comedy, musicals, Christian content, and many others. As you flip through, you skip content that are not interesting to you. It is also possible to engage and interact with people from many parts of the world.

Counselling and prayers.

It is good to see a counsellor for advice, or prayers, especially when the stress is emotional. Believers that seek counsel or prayer benefit immensely from these. It is also good to seek counsel from therapists, even though some of them are non-religious and may not be able to offer prayers. Intuitively, you would know what is best for you at any particular time.

CHAPTER 14

GENERAL OVERVIEW ON TEMPER MANAGEMENT

As individuals in different facets of our life journey, there are certain things in this journey, generally that we need to acknowledge, and allow to guide us.

Accept Jesus Christ

The first thing is to identify with tested and trusted principles over the centuries. The best lifestyle to adopt is the lifestyle of Jesus Christ. He says in Matthew 11:28,

"Come unto me, all ye that labour and are heavy laden, and I will give you rest"

When you live your life based on God's word, it guarantees you prosperity and good success (Joshua 1:8), and places you in the place of favour, that you life is like a tree, planted by the rivers of water. You will live a beautiful life, glorifying the name of God in everything that you do.

Repent from sin.

A sinner is always afraid about people and situations around him. The Bible says there is no peace for the wicked (Isaiah 48:22). Sin robs you of your peace, torments you, and makes you temperamental.

1 John 4:18

There is no fear in love; but perfect love casteth out fear: because fear hath torment. He that feareth is not made perfect in love.

A good decision is to be loving and kind hearted, while eschewing sin. Take this life easy, run from sin.

Forgiveness.

The bible encourages us to forbear and to forgive (Colossians 3:13). Sometimes, we may not commit sin, but people could offend us and provoke our temperament. If you are able to forgive, then you have great peace and tranquillity. A bad temper is done away with and every wall hitherto created between you and your helpers, and significant others collapse. The health benefits are numerous if you are able to forgive and heal internally.

The bible says also

2 Timothy 2:4

No man that warreth entangleth himself with the affairs of this life; that he may please him who hath chosen him to be a soldier.

Study and meditate in the word of God

The word of God is like a lamp unto our feet, that when we are lost in the darkness of this world, and are confused and jittery, the word of God illuminates our hearts and give us succour. The word of God according to 2 Timothy 3:16 says

2 Timothy 3:16

All scripture is given by inspiration of God, and is profitable for doctrine, for reproof, for correction, for instruction in righteousness:

Wherever you need reproof, correction, instruction, and doctrine, you will always find it in the word of God. There is no aspect of human challenges, that the bible does not have an answer to, if you study diligently.

Patience.

The act of being patient is a sterling quality that we must try as much as possible to cultivate. A patient person has a lot of time to think and order or reorder their priorities. A patient person is able to see what many other people are unable to see, and utilise them for their benefits.

On the other hand, some other people are not patient, and are therefore temperamental. The dabble into issues without thinking, and commit many errors which sometimes could be fatal. Patience is one of the fruits of the spirit, and God love's people who are patient.

Overcome fear and doubt.
Fear and doubt are two factors that could heighten your temper and make you react inappropriately. It is always good to have a good knowledge and understanding of spiritual things. When you are not sure, take it to the Lord in prayer, until you receive an answer from the Holy Spirit. Many people will continue to be victims of their circumstances and continue in fear, doubt, confusion and a poor temperament and bad outcomes, because they cannot patiently inquire from the Lord. It is also good to acquire secular knowledge in addition to spiritual knowledge, which is so powerful. Knowledge is power, and gives clarity.

Do everything possible to be successful.

Success is partly revelation, partly a mindset and lifestyle, as well as hard work. Failure in life is not a good thing, because it is frustrating, and impacts upon temper negatively. This is why we must have the mindset of a winner in everything we do, and strive to be excellent. Whatever that need to be done should be prayerfully put before God who formed us. He knows the beginning and the end, and the Holy Spirit cam make life very interesting, if we partner with him. Another thing is to be consistent in working hard, and problems will bow down to us and we shall be successful and happy.

Genetic.

It is well documented that temper issues could be inherited. Temper runs in some families to the extent that they commit different kinds of atrocities, which run in the family. When a thing like that happens, you need to go for deliverance, because it is in the genes. Spiritually, there are also demons that are responsible for such behaviour, and transmitting them from family to family.

Stress.

In a quest to make ends meet financially or socially, we engage in activities. Sometimes, unknown to us, we go beyond our abilities, physically and emotionally. At other times, we intentionally go beyond our capabilities, for rewards, financially or otherwise. We need to know however, that only the living can enjoy the pleasures of life, and we need to do things in moderation.

Matthew 16:26
For what is a man profited, if he shall gain the whole world, and lose his own soul? Or what shall a man give in exchange for his soul?

Whenever we are stretched beyond limits, we need to unwind and manage stress. The issue of stress management has been dealt with exhaustively in an earlier chapter.

Unfair treatment
In our dealings with people, there are rules and regulations that govern how we relate with people. This also brings about the subject of responsibilities. We all have responsibilities to ourselves, to our spouses, to our children, in our workplace, in our church, in our community, and to our nation. All these entities

should be adequately addressed, otherwise we would go wrong on certain planes, and generate a ripple of negative temperament. To avoid bad temperament, we have to follow the rules, and live up to our responsibilities.

A lot of sleep.

A lot of sleep is required to effect repairs physically and biochemically. The expected norm is eight hours of work, eight hours of leisure, and eight hours of sleep. Apart from physical and biochemical systems, the brain as an organ on its own needs a lot of sleep, and rest to function optimally. We should be sensitive to the demands of our biological systems. Most times, after a hard day's work, you get home and feel like eating and sleeping. This is not a time to engage in discussions or other things. Give your body what it is demanding from you. A lot of sleep, and you can cope with daily activities without any display of temper.

Financial problems.

Economists say that human needs are unlimited, but the resources are limited. In the light of this, human beings are frustrated when there is no Godliness and contentment (1

Timothy 6:6). Sometimes we do desire too many things than necessary. Many women struggle to buy clothing and trinkets that they hardly put on. Vanity of vanities saith the preacher, all is vanity (Ecclesiastes 1:2). Another issue is lack of planning. When you don't plan, you disorganise yourself. Everything needs to be planned, and you need a diary and organiser as well. By doing this, you make life easy for yourself, and avoid temper issues everywhere.

Marital problems.

The bible says that he that findeth a wife, findeth a good thing, and obtained the favour of the LORD (Proverbs 18:22). However, if we do not deal according to knowledge (1 Peter 3:7), our prayers could be hindered. When prayers are hindered, then you don't have what you want, and you are temperamental. Everyone in marriage need to carry out their responsibilities to one another, and don't hurt one another. Marriage should foster love and companionship, and not to torment. We also need to teach our children, morally, so that they can give us peace.

Triumphing over illness and disability

There are lots of challenges that arise with illness and disability. The things you earnestly wish you could do are now within your reach, as you depend on people for your living. Many of these people have their own concerns, and may not be always available. This makes you to think about your predicaments, and you may be jittery many times, leading to a bad temper. This heightened temperament could hinder the help you may be able to receive and reduce your quality of life. In times of illness, you need to empathise with your carers, because they have concerns. Also try to explain and make your situation very clear for people to be able to understand you. Always have a thank you attitude to people, and you will see the sense of satisfaction jump in you, with your helpers willing to do more. In your bed of sickness, watch movies, read books and play games amongst others.

Academic problems

The major source of pride in the youth is their academic attainment. If for any reason, there are problems academically, their will be issues related to academic progress, it can mean so much to a youngster. Strategies aimed at academic progress include planning and having g a timetable, look for a mentor, learn to collaborate with students to do group studies. There may be a need for a Counsellor.

Prioritise your finances

There could be overbearing responsibilities on a person in several ways, in carrying out our responsibilities. A man for example may have overbearing financial responsibilities in meeting the needs of his wife and children. If the members of the extended family also expect him to meet a need, then continuously, this becomes Overbearing, making him to react with a bad temperament. Everyone should not keep promises that will give them stress, or affect their health. You should also try to prioritise your expenditure at any point in time.

Find something to do

There is the problem of employment all over the world, which may impact upon your temperament and your health. Too much of emotional stress and worries associated with thinking about the solution to the problems. Whilst waiting for a paid job, take up something that will occupy you and douse your temperament, build your curriculum vitae, and maintain your health status. Also, it helps to take up an available job even if the renumeration is not exactly what you are expecting. It is better than not having a job at all. Hunger and suffering are not our good friends. If there is no support from family, and you are unemployed continuously, suffering is bound to come.

Genetic issues

A genetic issue in spiritual terms is causes by an inherited demon. Based on understanding, a phenomenon may have a spiritual or scientific explanation. For example, a genetic disease (2 Kings 5:27) is as a result of a generational curse, but the doctor says its a genetic problem and is incurable. However, we know that genetic problems could be overcome by deliverance prayers. Likewise, mental illnesses. To break the yoke of genetic disorders, the approach of deliverance is the best, though this is not to say that medical intervention is totally irrelevant. If you are delivered from a demon provoking your temperament, then you are delivered from negative temperaments.

Overcoming the shock of bereavement.
Bereavement is inevitable sometimes, at least of an aged parent. When this happens, depending on relationship and attachment, there is some form of depression, and shock. This is associated with a jittery attitude and snappy temper too. It is good to understand that except by a miracle, nothing can be done to reverse what has happened. A bereaved person should not be overburdened by a crowd and too many visits, but needs sometime to reflect and stabilise emotionally. A few close

associates may need to be with a bereaved person to keep them company.

Housing problems

A homeless person is an emotionally unstable person, because that condition is also associated with unemployment, poverty and lack, and homeless people are vulnerable to infectious diseases, and physical attacks with fear. In some cultures, you may have family members or friends to take you in with them. In some other cultures, you may have access to council housing if you are patient enough. The best approach is to try and get something to do, in the form of work, or learn something new and rewarding. Gradually it takes your emotional problems away, as you can also get some money for yourself.

Printed in Great Britain
by Amazon